PIANO / VOCAL / GUITAR

I AM... SASHA FIERCE

ISBN 978-1-4234-7574-3

HAL•LEONARD®
CORPORATION

7777 W. BLUEMOUND RD. P.O. BOX 13819 MILWAUKEE, WI 53213

Visit Hal Leonard Online at
www.halleonard.com

IF I WERE A BOY

Words and Music by TOBY GAD
and BRITTANY CARLSON

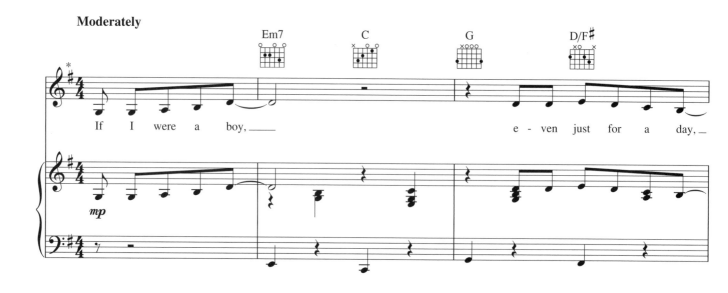

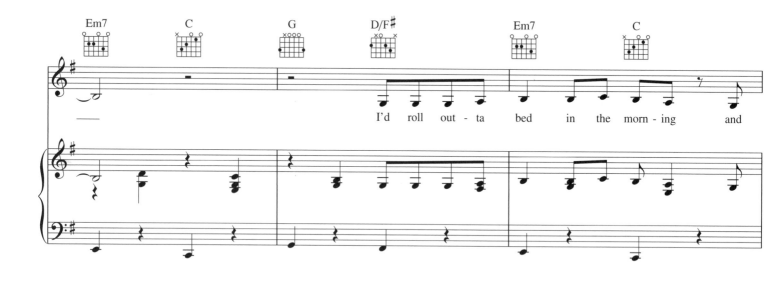

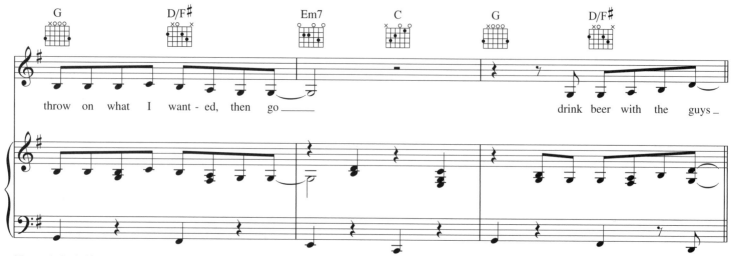

*Recorded a half step lower.

HALO

Words and Music by BEYONCÉ KNOWLES,
RYAN TEDDER and EVAN BOGART

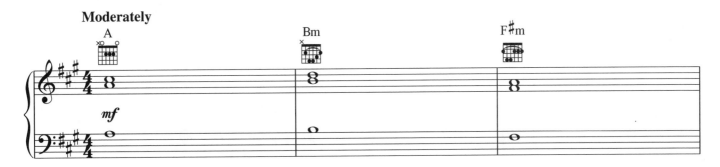

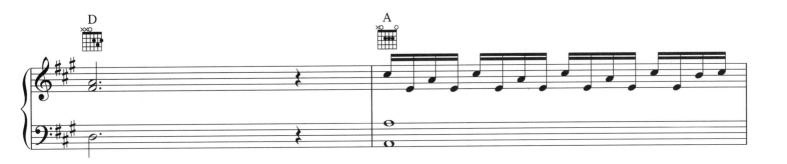

Re-mem-ber those walls I built?

*Verse one is written an octave higher than sung.

Lead vocal sung both times at written pitch.

Ev -'ry-where I'm look - in' now,_

DISAPPEAR

Words and Music by BEYONCÉ KNOWLES, IAN DENCH,
DAVE McCRACKEN, HUGO CHAKRABONGSE
and AMANDA GHOST

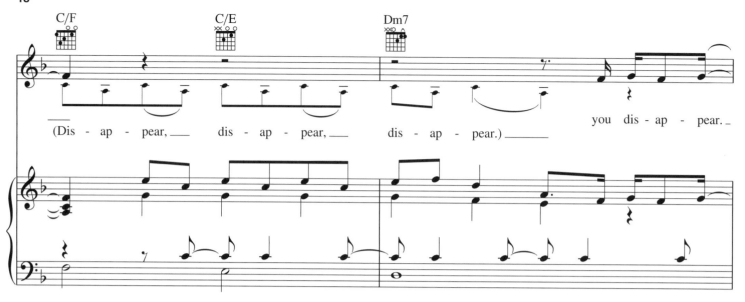

and my heart stays ___ faith - ful. ___

And time has come and time has passed, ___ if it's good it's got to last, ___

D.S. al Coda

it felt so right. ___

BROKENHEARTED GIRL

Words and Music by BEYONCÉ KNOWLES,
TOR ERIK HERMANSEN, MIKKEL ERIKSEN
and KENNETH EDMONDS

AVE MARIA

Words and Music by BEYONCÉ KNOWLES,
MAKEBA RIDDICK, TOR ERIK HERMANSEN,
AMANDA GHOST, MIKKEL ERIKSEN
and IAN DENCH

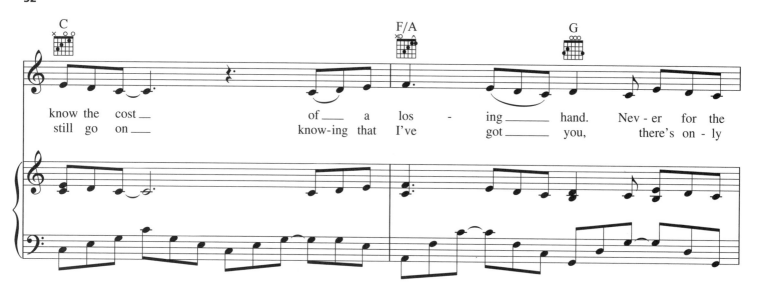

know the cost ___ of ___ a los - ing ___ hand. Nev - er for the
still go on ___ know-ing that I've got ___ you, there's on - ly

grace of ___ God, oh I, ___ I found ___
us when the lights go down. ___ You are my

heav - en on ___ earth, you are my last, my ___ first, and then I
heav - en on ___ earth, you are my hun - ger, my ___ thirst. I al - ways

SMASH INTO YOU

Words and Music by BEYONCÉ KNOWLES,
CHRISTOPHER STEWART and TERIUS NASH

* *Recorded a half-step lower*

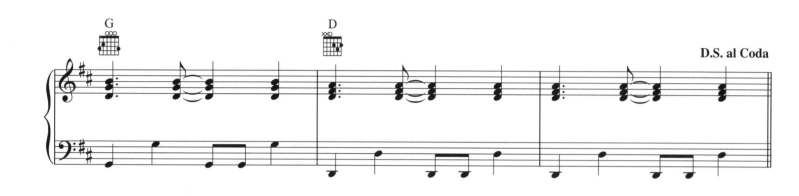

D.S. al Coda

CODA

I'm   soaked in your love, __   and love _____ was

right in my path, __ in my grasp. __ And you _____ and me __ be - long. __

SATELLITES

Words and Music by BEYONCÉ KNOWLES,
DAVE McCRACKEN, IAN DENCH
and AMANDA GHOST

THAT'S WHY YOU'RE BEAUTIFUL

Words and Music by BEYONCÉ KNOWLES,
JAMES FAUNTLEROY II and ANDREW HEY

ba - by, ___ and that's why you're beau - ti - ful. ___ I'm not won-der-ing why ___

A/G   D6/F#   Gmaj7   Bm7   A

___ the sky's blue, ___ that's not ___ my busi - ness. All I know is I ___

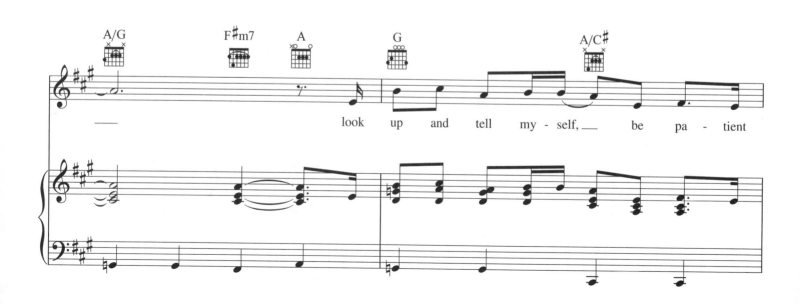

A/G   F#m7   A   G   A/C#

___ look up and tell my - self, ___ be pa - tient

love,   it could be us. _____

And lov - ers ____ used ___ to make love _____ and died just ___ to give us ____

look up and tell my-self, ___ be pa - tient

love, that could be us. ___

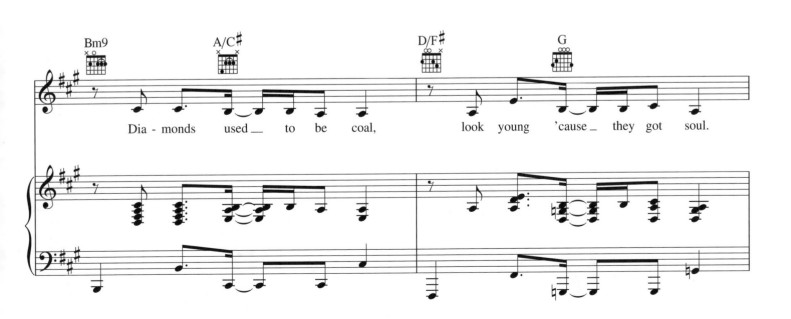

Dia - monds used ___ to be coal, look young 'cause ___ they got soul.

Bm9
A/C♯
D/F♯
G
And my heart used to be cold
'til your hands laid on my soul.
Bm9
Cmaj7
Some-bod - y's got to stay deep in love,
that could be us,
G
Dmaj9
4fr
that's why we're beau - ti - ful,
that's why you're beau - ti - ful.

That's why you're beau - ti - ful, _____ that's why you're beau - ti - ful, ____

____ that's why you're beau - ti - ful. _____

SINGLE LADIES
(Put a Ring on It)

Words and Music by BEYONCÉ KNOWLES,
THADDIS HARRIS, CHRISTOPHER STEWART
and TERIUS NASH

Moderate groove

All _ the sin-gle la-dies, _ all _ the sin-gle la-dies. _ All _ the

sin-gle la-dies, _ all _ the sin-gle la-dies. _ All _ the sin-gle la-dies, _ all _ the sin-gle la-dies. _ All _ the

sin-gle la-dies, _ now put your hands up.

Up in the club, we just broke up. I'm
gloss for my lips, a man on my hips, hold me

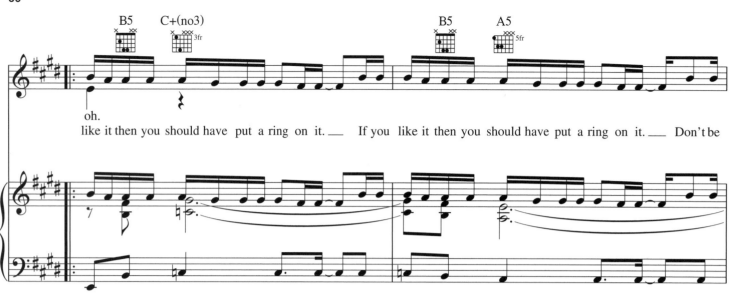

oh.

like it then you should have put a ring on it. __ If you like it then you should have put a ring on it. __ Don't be

mad _ once you see __ that he want it. __ If you like it then you should have put a ring on it. Oh, oh, 'Cause if you

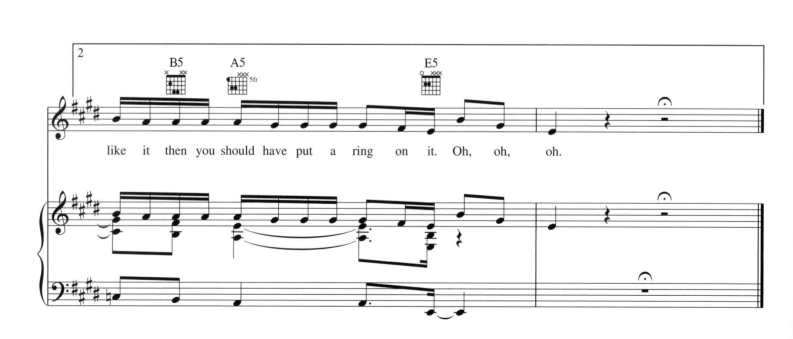

like it then you should have put a ring on it. Oh, oh, oh.

RADIO

Words and Music by BEYONCÉ KNOWLES,
JAMES SCHEFFER, RICHARD BUTLER
and DWAYNE NESMITH

With energy

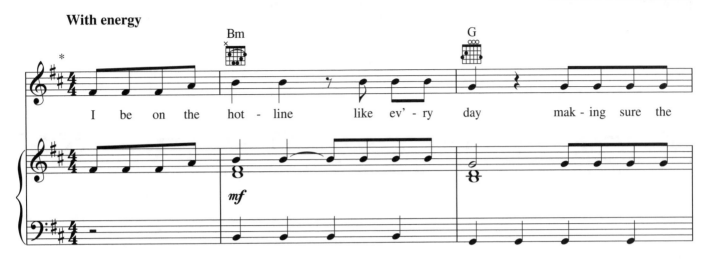

I be on the hot-line like ev'-ry day mak-ing sure the

D. J. know what I want him to play. You know I got my top back and my beat

low-ow, rock-ing my stun-ner shades and turn-ing up my ra-di - o - o, turn up my ra-di-

* Recorded a half-step lower

67

DIVA

Words and Music by BEYONCÉ KNOWLES,
SHONDRAE CRAWFORD and SEAN GARRETT

Moderate hip-hop groove

CODA

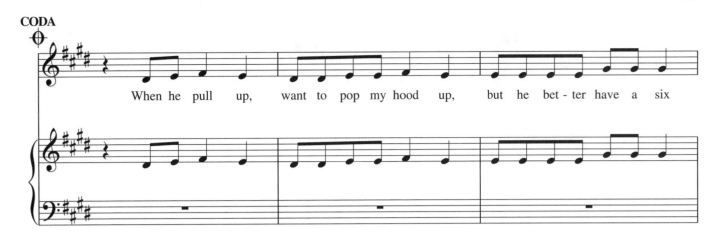

When he pull up, want to pop my hood up, but he bet-ter have a six

pack in the cool-er. Get-ting mon-ey, di-vas get-ting mon-ey, if you

ain't get-ting mon-ey then you ain't got noth-ing for me. Tell me some-thing, where your

boss at? Where my la-dies up in there that like to talk back? I want to

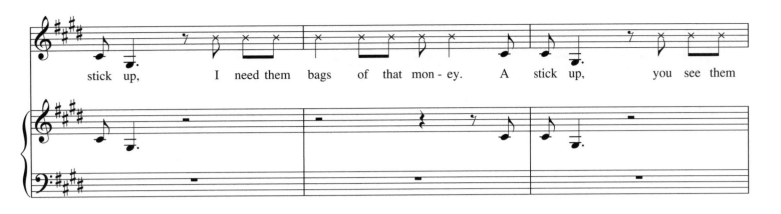

stick up, I need them bags of that mon- ey. A stick up, you see them

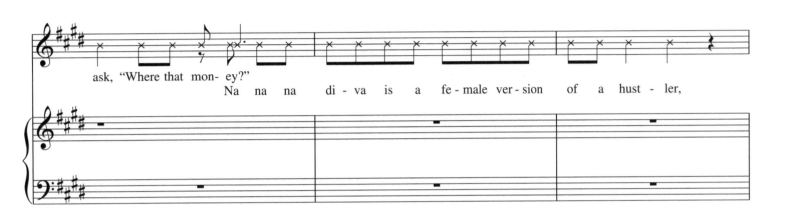

ask, "Where that mon- ey?" Na na na di - va is a fe - male ver - sion of a hust - ler,

of a hust - ler, of a, of a hust - ler. Na na na di - va is a fe - male ver - sion

of a hust - ler, of a hust - ler, of a, of a hust - ler.

I'm a, a di - va, I'm a, I'm a a di - va. I'm a,

I'm a, a di - va, I'm a, I'm a, a di - va. I'm a,

I'm a, a di - va, I'm a, I'm a a di - va. I'm a,

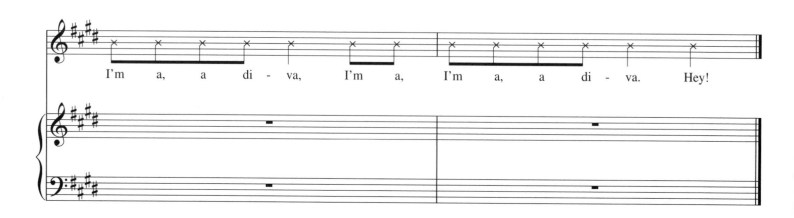

I'm a, a di - va, I'm a, I'm a, a di - va. Hey!

SWEET DREAMS

Words and Music by BEYONCÉ KNOWLES,
JAMES SCHEFFER, RICHARD BUTLER, JR.
and WAYNE WILKINS

Moderate groove

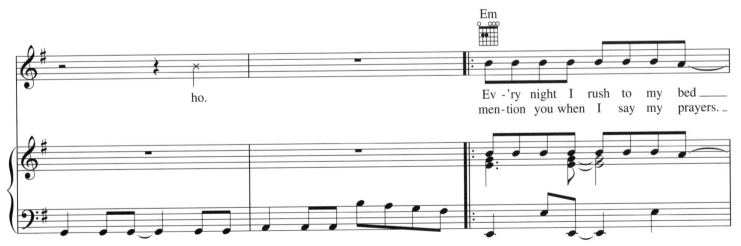

* *Recorded a half step lower.*

VIDEO PHONE

Words and Music by BEYONCÉ KNOWLES,
ANGELA BEYINCE, SHONDRAE CRAWFORD
and SEAN GARRETT

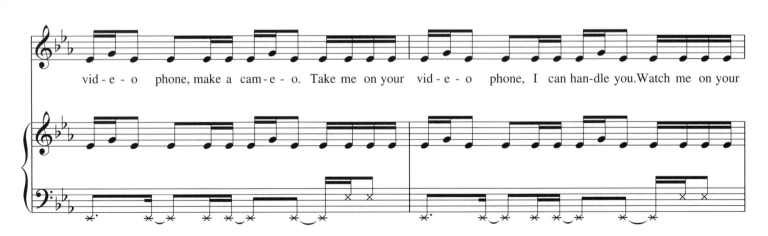

Ba-by, you're do-ing some-thing right, _ you just can-celed ev-'ry oth-er man here. You

say you like my bag and the col-or of my nails, you can see that I've got it go-ing on. I

want to make sure you re-mem-ber me, _ so I'm-a leave my num-ber on your vid-e-o phone. _

I've got no time for front - ing, _ I know just what I'm want - ing. _

D.S. al Coda

So take your pic-ture on my vid-e-o phone,_ you can pick your own song_ and you could be the on-ly one._

_ I know you_ like_ that,_ turn you in-to a star, I got it_ like_ that._

Ba-by don't_ fight it_ 'cause when I miss your call I hit you_ right_ back_ on my

vid-e-o phone._ Them hust-lers keep on talk - ing, they like the way I'm

pop - ping   You're say-ing that you   want _ me,   press   re-cord, ba - by, film   On your

me.
vid - e - o   phone, make a cam-e - o. Take me on your   vid - e - o   phone, I can han-dle you. Watch me on your

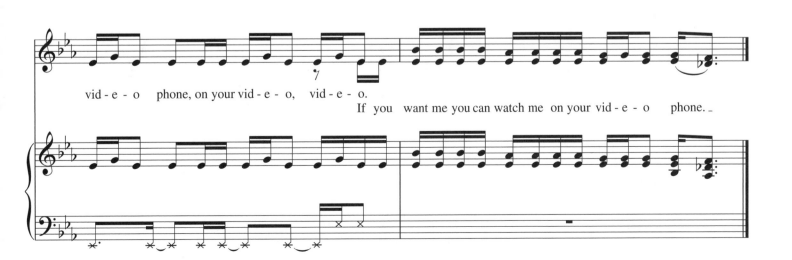

vid - e - o   phone, on your vid - e - o, vid - e - o.
                                          If you   want me you can watch me on your vid - e - o   phone. _

HELLO

Words and Music by BEYONCÉ KNOWLES,
DAVID QUINONES, EVAN BOGART
and RAMON OWEN

In a fast six

Oh.

Oh. _____

I love to see you walk in-to a room, bod-y shin-ing, light-ing up the place.
I get so ex-cit-ed ba-by when you trav-el with me when I'm on my grind.

* Recorded a half-step lower.

EGO

Words and Music by BEYONCÉ KNOWLES,
ELVIS WILLIAMS and HAROLD LILLY, JR.

*Recorded a half step lower.

SCARED OF LONELY

Words and Music by BEYONCÉ KNOWLES,
RODNEY JERKINS, LaSHAWN DANIELS,
RICHARD BUTLER, CRYSTAL JOHNSON
and SOLANGE KNOWLES

POISON

Words and Music by BEYONCÉ KNOWLES,
TOR ERIK HERMANSEN, MIKKEL ERIKSEN
and JOHNTA AUSTIN

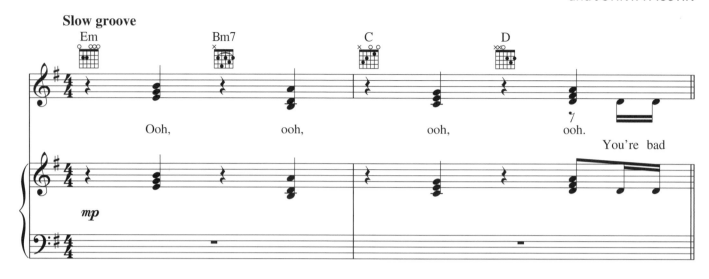

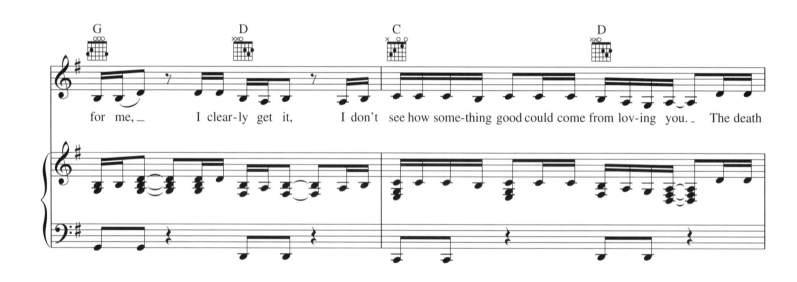